The Devil

IN SALEM VILLAGE

THE DEVIL IN SALEM VILLAGE

The Story of
THE SALEM WITCHCRAFT TRIALS

LAUREL VAN DER LINDE

Spotlight on American History
The Millbrook Press • Brookfield, Connecticut

Cover photograph "The Trial of George Jacobs, August 5, 1692" painted by T. H. Matteson courtesy Essex Institute, Salem, Mass.

Photographs courtesy of: The New York Historical Society: p. 8; The Bettmann Archive: p. 16; New York Public Library Picture Collection: p. 19; The Granger Collection: pp. 22, 27, 31, 39, 55, 60; Danvers Archival Center: pp. 24, 64; Library of Congress: p. 34; Essex Institute: pp. 40, 44 (top right and bottom), 49 (right); The Harvard University Portrait Collection, Cambridge, Mass.: p. 44 (top left); Court of Oyer and Terminer, Deposition of Ann Putnam jr. against Sarah Good, 1692 (on deposit at the Essex Institute, Salem, Mass.). Courtesy of James D. Leary, Clerk of Courts for Essex County: p. 49 (left)

Library of Congress Cataloging-in-Publication Data

Van der Linde, Laurel, 1952–
The Devil in Salem Village : the story of the Salem witchcraft trials / by Laurel van der Linde.
p.   cm.—(Spotlight on American history)
Includes bibliographical references (p.   ) and index.
Summary: Describes the panic that swept through colonial Salem, Massachusetts, when the people were convinced that witches were among them, and outlines the factors leading up to this episode.
ISBN 1-56294-144-5
1. Witchcraft—Massachusetts—Salem—Juvenile literature.
2. Trials (Witchcraft)—Massachusetts—Salem—Juvenile literature.
[1. Witchcraft—Massachusetts—Salem.   2. Trials (Witchcraft)—Massachusetts—Salem.   3. Salem (Mass.)—History—Colonial period, ca. 1600–1775.] I. Title. II. Series.
BF1756.V36 1992
133.4′3′097445—dc20   91-24403 CIP AC

Contents

For Gower

A woman condemned as a witch is led to execution.

1

A DEADLY GAME

Sarah Good stood on the wooden platform of Gallows Hill, her hands tied, a rope around her neck. Nicholas Noyes, minister of the First Church of Salem, asked her one last time to confess to the crime of witchcraft. "You are a liar," she replied. "I am no more a witch than you are a wizard. And if you kill me, God will give you blood to drink." The minister signaled the hangman to release the floor of the platform. Sarah Good, along with four other condemned witches, was hanged by the neck until dead.

The execution of Sarah Good, Rebecca Nurse, Elizabeth How, Susanna Martin, and Sarah Wilds on July 19, 1692, was the second resulting from the Salem witchcraft trials. The first, also a hanging, had been that of Bridget Bishop on June 10. This dark and frightening episode in America's early colonial history ran its course throughout the year of 1692. Before it was over, more than two hundred people had been accused of witchcraft. One hundred and forty-one were jailed, including Dorcas Good, the five-year-old daughter of Sarah Good. Two of the accused witches died in prison while awaiting trial. One man was tortured to death. Nineteen men and women were tried, convicted, and executed, along with two dogs. The panic was not confined to Salem but spread to the neighboring communities of Beverly, Amesbury, and Andover.

This madness began with the overactive imaginations of two little girls, aged nine and eleven.

Elizabeth (Betty) Parris and her older cousin Abigail Williams had come to the Massachusetts Bay colony of Salem Village in 1689, when Betty's father, the Reverend Samuel Parris, accepted a position there as parish minister. The Parris family brought with them two slaves from the West Indies, John Indian and his wife, Tituba.

Winters in Salem Village were hard and long. The children were forced to spend most of their time indoors. Equally confining was the Puritan religion by which they were raised. Rarely did they get out of the house except to go to Sunday services. Girls in particular were expected to dress and act like little adults, limiting their activities to sewing, churning the butter, and reciting their Bible lessons.

Mrs. Parris's duties as the minister's wife frequently called her away from the parsonage, so the slave Tituba was given charge not only of the housekeeping but of Betty and Abigail as well. Hoping to relieve their boredom, Tituba began to tell the girls stories of magic and sorcery from her native island of Barbados. She played at fortune-telling, making a crude crystal ball by dropping the white of an egg into a glass of water. Of course, Betty and Abigail knew these activities were strictly forbidden; Betty had heard her father preach against them often enough. But their curiosity overcame them. It wasn't long before the news of Tituba's "little sorceries" had secretly spread to three other girls living nearby. Eagerly, they joined Betty and Abigail in the Parris kitchen. None could have had any idea of the deathly consequences of their games.

COMPARED WITH other witch-hunts, the Salem trials were not notable for the number of people executed. Thousands had been hanged or burned as witches in England and other European countries the century before. There had also been other witchcraft trials in the American colonies before the Salem outbreak. What is important about Salem is that it was the largest witch-hunt in America. It also marked the end of three centuries of witch-hunts in Europe and the American colonies. In Salem, people who had led blameless lives suddenly found themselves not only accused of witchcraft but jailed, tried, and convicted.

There was no real evidence against these people; just the made-up stories of the hysterical "circle girls"—Betty Parris, Abigail Williams, and others—who claimed that the witches' "shapes" had tried to get them to sign the "Devil's book." When they refused, the girls said, these "shapes" hurt them by sticking pins into their flesh. Some of the neighbors of the accused saw the trials as a good way to end neighborhood disagreements and added their imagined stories to those of the girls. In that way, they were able to get rid of a troublesome neighbor.

The accused witches were not allowed any legal help and had to face eight judges alone. The trials operated on the belief that an accused person was guilty until proved innocent. Just being accused was a sign of guilt. The only way to escape the hangman's noose was to confess, for the Puritans would not hang a confessing witch. More than fifty people did confess to crimes they could not possibly have committed.

Several others managed to escape prison and go into hiding in other towns until the madness was over. Two convicted women were not executed because they were pregnant. By the time they had their babies, the trials had ended. They were pardoned and released from prison along with others who had not yet been tried. It is to the credit of those who were executed that they stood by the truth.

And just what was their crime? Today we think of witches mostly at Halloween, as old women dressed in long, black robes and tall, pointed hats—ugly, perhaps, but really harmless. It is hard to understand that some of the best and most educated minds of Salem in the late 1600s so sincerely believed in witches that they sent people to their deaths. But that is exactly what they did.

The Salem witches were tried and executed under the biblical passage "Thou shalt not suffer a witch to live." But even the Bible, which was the cornerstone of the Puritan faith, does not define a witch. How, then, did this belief begin? And how did it get so out of control?

2

AN ANCIENT
BEGINNING

The roots of witchcraft lie in the practices of ancient religions. In the earliest farming communities, survival depended strictly on the crops that were harvested each year. In their thinking, these early peoples eventually linked the fields, which produced crops, with the tribal women, who produced children. As a result, their most important god was a woman, the Great Mother Goddess. Although she was called by many different names, this belief in the Great Mother was central to many ancient cultures at the early stages of their individual development.

In most of these societies, a wise old priestess led her people in their worship of the Great Mother. She possessed knowledge of animal and herb lore with the "magical" powers to both heal and harm. Nature was sacred to the old religion. Ceremonies were held in forests and caves. People dressed in animal skins to enact a successful hunt, and special herbal drinks were brewed to be used in the rituals. Many of the followers of the old ways practiced astrology and believed they could predict the future.

Over the centuries, as methods of war and weaponry developed, men became more important. Stories of war heroes made them into near gods, and religions centered on male gods grew alongside that of the Great Mother. Followers of the new religions viewed the followers of the old with less and less understanding. The new religions of the Greeks, Romans, and, eventually, the Christians were suspicious of the ceremonial herbal drinks, believing them to be magic potions. They thought the person wearing animal skins in the hunting ritual actually changed shape and became an animal, and they feared anyone who could look in the future. From this clash between the old and new religions began the belief in witchcraft.

The final conflict between religions occurred with the spread of Christianity to Ireland and Britain. Around the fifth century A.D., these two countries still followed the belief of the Great Mother Goddess. In Ireland, the Brigantes worshiped the goddess Brigid. So deeply rooted was this ancient religion that Pope Gregory soon realized that Christianity could not overthrow the ancient rites. He instructed his priests to include these rituals with Christian ceremonies. As a result, the Mother Goddess, Brigid, became Saint Bridget, and early Christian churches were built in the same places that had been sacred to the old religion.

In England, the worship of the goddess Ceridwen was led by priests and priestesses called Druids. It was thought that these priests and priestesses could control the weather, heal the sick, and cast spells or brew potions that would cause either love or hardship. All of these abilities later became associated with witches.

The English beliefs had a direct bearing on the events in Salem in 1692. In order to become a witch, it was believed, an individual had to make a pact with the Devil. In exchange for that person's immortal soul, the Devil would then grant his or her wishes. The Devil would place a "Devil's mark" on his chosen to seal the agreement and secure the new witch's pledge of service to him. The Devil supposedly made the mark himself, with his claw, in a hidden place, such as under the eyelids or in the armpits. The marks were given at the end of initiation rites that were held at meetings called sabbats. The belief was that sabbats took place at night, in mountains, forests, or caves. After "services" of Devil worship, there would be feasting and dancing, with the witches flying home before dawn, usually on broomsticks.

Witches were organized into groups called covens. Each coven consisted of thirteen people: twelve witches and a leader. The leader of the coven was usually a man who represented the Devil by dressing in animal skins and horns when he conducted the sabbats. Although women were more often accused of witchcraft than were men, men could be witches, too. A male witch was sometimes called a wizard.

The Devil would also assign a new member a "familiar." Familiars were supposedly demons of lower rank who would assume the shape of a common animal, such as a cat or dog or bird. Black cats in particular were thought to be familiars. Witches were said to use their familiars to assist them in bewitching their victims. Familiars, it was believed, fed off the blood of the witch. During the Salem witchcraft trials, the bodies of the accused witches were searched for a "witch's mark," a spot where it was thought the familiar would suck the witch's blood. Any mark—a mole, a birthmark, a freckle—was enough to get a person hanged.

Witches and Broomsticks

THE PICTURE of a witch flying overhead on her broomstick is a common one. In fact, the association of broomsticks and witches goes back to ancient times. During spring planting ceremonies, the worshipers of the Great Mother would mount brooms and pitchforks and ride them like hobbyhorses through the fields.

Broomsticks are mostly associated with female witches. This is probably because the broom has long been a woman's tool and, therefore, became a feminine symbol. At the time of the Salem witchcraft trials, a broom was propped outside the front door as a sign to callers that the woman of the house was not at home.

Some folklore held that the Devil gave a broom and magic "flying ointment" to all new witches as part of their initiation. Supposedly, witches rode their brooms to sabbats, carrying their familiars with them. And sometimes they even rode them out to sea to stir up storms. It was thought that the newer witches frequently fell off the broomsticks. On nights when sabbats were believed to be held, townspeople and farmers would set out pitchforks to kill any witches who fell off their brooms while flying over the fields.

THE FEAR OF WITCHES brought about witch-hunts that reached a peak in Europe during the three centuries between 1450 and 1750. In the 1480s, Pope Innocent VIII, thinking that not enough witches were being punished, asked two Germans of the Dominican Order, Heinrich Kramer and James Sprenger, to help him eliminate witches in northern Germany. They wrote a kind of witch-hunter's handbook, called the *Malleus Maleficarum*, that described witches and their behavior. It gave guidelines on how to accuse, try, and punish a witch. The *Malleus Maleficarum* was published in Germany in 1486 and quickly became a best-seller, second only to the Bible. Its popularity quickly spread to other countries, particularly France and Italy. There was even a pocket-size edition, so judges could refer to it easily in court.

The *Malleus Maleficarum* stated that "common justice demands that a witch should not be condemned to death unless she is convicted by her own confession." In order to obtain that confession, the book offered several methods of "encouragement." First, the witch's body was examined for both a Devil's mark and a witch's mark. Because the witch's mark was said to be used to feed the witch's familiar, it was thought to be insensitive to pain. Consequently, the witch's mark was pricked with a long pin or needle. If the victim showed no sign of pain and the prick drew no blood, that was evidence that he or she was a witch.

Another practice was "waking," in which the accused was not allowed to sleep until he or she confessed. Similar was "walking," in which the victim was walked back and forth until he or she collapsed and confessed. "Swimming" was also common. The supposed witch was bound hand and foot and thrown into water. If the victim floated, he or she was a witch. If the person sank, that was proof of innocence. There was no guarantee, however, that a person who sank would be pulled from the water before drowning.

"Swimming," or the water test, was based on the belief that water would reject a witch. If the accused person sank, he or she was innocent.

Accused witches were also routinely flogged, burned, and branded. Sometimes the family of the victim was tortured in an effort to obtain a confession. The more accused witches resisted confessing, the more it was taken as a sign that the Devil was aiding them.

These and other methods recommended by the *Malleus Male-ficarum* were used during the course of European and American witchcraft trials.

England, in particular, had a direct effect on the methods later used to hunt and try witches in the New World. (The very word *witch* comes from the Anglo-Saxon *wicce,* meaning "sorceress.") English witchcraft laws were eventually used in the Salem witchcraft trials. A book published in 1597, *Daemonologie,* became a kind of textbook on the subject of witchcraft. And a witchcraft act passed in England in 1603 called for the death penalty for any act of sorcery, whether or not the supposed victim had died.

These, then, were the attitudes and beliefs that people settling the English colonies brought with them to the New World.

3

SEVENTEENTH-CENTURY SALEM

Six years after the landing of the *Mayflower,* Salem was founded by an Englishman, Roger Conant, in 1626. Located fifteen miles from Boston, the site he chose had a natural harbor and riverways leading inland that made it a good place to build a trading post and start a fishing station. The name "Salem" was taken from the Hebrew word *shalom,* meaning "peace." Little did the citizens of Salem realize how much that peace would be shattered by the events of 1692.

There were actually two Salems in 1692: Salem Town and the farming community of Salem Village. Within four years of its founding, the town of Salem had outgrown its original boundaries. Salem's citizens soon realized that they could not grow enough food to support themselves on the existing site. So they began to move away from the harbor and build farms farther inland. This was the

A Puritan couple on their way to church.

beginning of Salem Village. It was in Salem Village (now Danvers) that the witchcraft trials began.

Because it was located right next to Salem Town, Salem Village was still considered to be part of the town. The farmers of the village had to pay taxes to Salem Town and, because of the threat of Indian raids, help with the night watch. The people of Salem Village were expected to attend Sunday services in the town. For those villagers whose farms were at the farthest end of Salem Village, this was a hardship. The distance to the center of Salem Town was as much as twelve miles. Traveling this distance in the 1600s could take half a day. In addition, the Indians were a constant worry. Rare was the father who did not carry a gun as he escorted his family to Sunday meeting.

Understandably, the people of Salem Village wanted to separate from Salem Town. But Salem Town did not want to lose its much-needed farming community; it depended on the village to produce its food. The farmers, however, persisted and petitioned the town council for permission to build their own church and have their own minister. Finally, the council agreed, and Salem Village was able to build its own meetinghouse in 1674. Salem Village was still not completely on its own, however. It would not be a separate town for another seventy-eight years.

*I*N THE SEVENTEENTH CENTURY, both Salem Town and Salem Village were surrounded by rocks, swamps, and forests. The farmers shared a common interest in the woods, pastures, and meadows. Each farmer usually had a horse, a cow, and perhaps a few pigs and goats. Wealth was determined mostly by how many animals a family owned.

[23]

The First Meeting House in Salem Village, built in 1674.

The village itself had a network of streets that were eight feet wide—wide enough for "foot, horse and cart." These narrow streets all led to Main Street. Main Street ran directly by the lifeblood of the Puritan community: the church, or meetinghouse.

So important was the church to daily life that a citizen of the town could not vote or hold any kind of office without being a member of the church in good standing. To not attend Sunday services and Communion was actually against the law. Where one sat in church on Sundays was a subject of much discussion. People sat in assigned pews, and those assignments were the cause of much jealousy. Men and women were not permitted to sit together. Rather, the men sat on one side, the women on the other. There was no heat in the church; even the comfort of portable foot stoves, which carried warm coals, was frowned upon.

The Puritan dress was somber. Individual tastes were over-ruled by the majority—style was determined by the church membership. As someone was always trying to change the fashion, the matter was constantly put to a vote. Lace or silk collars were outlawed, and something as simple as the width of the brim of a man's hat had to be voted on.

The Puritans chose first names that constantly reminded them of the God they worshiped. Names such as Stand-Fast Stringer, Be-Faithful Join, Weep-Not Billings, Increase Mather, Safety-in-Heaven Snat, and Kill-Sin Pimple were not uncommon. The rural Puritans referred to each other as "Goodwife" and "Goodman." "Goodwife" was shortened to "Goody," as in Goody Proctor or Goody Osburne. The more formal titles of "Mr." and "Mrs." were reserved for such persons as the minister and the governor and their wives.

The Puritan code was strict. Sins of omission weighed just as heavily as sins of commission. In other words, it was just as sinful to not do something right as it was to do something wrong. If a member of the community sinned, the Puritans believed that God would "even the score" and find a punishment to fit the crime. For example, if someone developed a toothache, that meant the person had been sinning with his or her teeth.

The Puritans tried to follow this line in creating appropriate punishments when a law was broken. Fines were given for such offenses as wearing a silk hood or lace sleeves, swearing, and drunkenness. For more serious crimes, such as burglary, the offender might be ordered to sit in the stocks in the town square, or be whipped and branded with the first letter of the crime he or she had committed. Sometimes tongues were cleaved (split), and sometimes ears were cut off. It depended on the crime and how severely the magistrates felt the offender should be punished.

Still, given the standards of punishment for this time, the Puritans would be considered merciful. When the Puritans left England in 1630, that country listed on its books a total of 223 crimes that were punishable by death. The most brutal of these crimes were punished by the most brutal of deaths. The Puritans reduced the number of capital offenses to fourteen and chose death on the gallows as suitable punishment. Hangings, in fact, were one of the few "outings" allowed Puritan children. Parents felt that it was good for the children to witness the results of sinful behavior.

Puritan parents also exposed their children to a gloomy view of death. The inscriptions found on Puritan tombstones are a good example of the Puritan view of death:

> *As you are, so were we*
> *As we are, so you shall be.*

and:

> *Death is a debt to nature due,*
> *I've paid the debt, and so must you.*

There were very few real doctors available, so the Puritans devised their own methods for curing common ailments. An almanac of the seventeenth century lists the following cures:

> *To cure sore eyes, catch a live frog*
> *and lick its eyes with your tongue.*

*Some lawbreakers were punished by being forced to sit
in the stocks, where townspeople could mock them.*

To cure stomach ache, inhale the cold breath of a duck.

A medicine to make a man's hair grow when he is bald. Take some fire flies and some red worms and black snails and some honey bees and dry them and then pound them into powder and mix them in milk or water and rub them on where the hair ought to be.

Education was equally scarce. There were a few private schools that taught reading, writing, and arithmetic. There were no public schools, however, and less than half the population could read or write. As education was so rare, the church ministers and town magistrates were considered the source of all wisdom.

THE PURITANS first came to America so that they might worship God in their own way. Oddly enough, however, neither tolerance nor pity was part of the Puritan religion. If one member of the community fell upon hard times, the Puritans would not offer help. They felt that a person's misfortune was ordered by God. To try to better one's lot in life was seen as defying God's will. As a result, there were many beggars in Salem Village. Most of these beggars were women who had been widowed. Some of them were insane.

Insanity was considered a sign of the Devil, and the Devil was very real to the Puritan mind. It was the Devil, after all, who was the cause of thunder and lightning. All persons were thought to be fighting an ongoing battle for the salvation of their souls. Although God limited Satan's powers, he did allow Satan to tempt his believers. It was thought that Satan selected the weakest to be his followers—in particular women, children, and the old and feeble-minded. Of course, any follower of the Devil was a witch. To doubt the existence of witchcraft was to doubt the existence of the Devil. To doubt the existence of the Devil was to doubt the existence of God.

The Puritans were a superstitious group. Sometimes a cross was scratched on the bells worn by the cows, or a piece of red flannel was tied around their necks, to help protect the livestock from evil spirits. Horseshoes were sometimes hung over doors to keep away evil spirits. These practices led to trouble during the hysteria of 1692. In one case, the fact that an accused witch hung a horseshoe above the door of her house weighed against her during her trial—it was thought that she relied on the horseshoe's magic power, rather than God, to fend off evil.

There had been other witchcraft trials in Massachusetts before those in Salem in 1692, some as far back as 1646 and others as late as 1683. The later trials involved some of the same people who either were accused of witchcraft or stood in judgment of those accused in 1692. At the time of the outbreak of the Salem witchcraft trials, the clergy and the magistrates feared deeply that they had been too merciful in their handling of past cases of witchcraft.

4

THE AFFLICTED

Salem Village was preparing for Thanksgiving. The younger members of the village were looking forward to the holiday. It was the last festive occasion of the year in the Puritan calendar. Christmas was not celebrated. The Puritans considered it a practice created strictly by and for Roman Catholics. So it happened, in November of 1691, that sixteen-year-old Mary Walcott took some of her mother's freshly baked pumpkin pies to the Parris parsonage to add to the stock for the Thanksgiving feast. When she entered the kitchen, she was surprised by what she found.

The slave Tituba was telling a story to Betty Parris and her cousin Abigail Williams. Abigail was held in rapt attention. Betty, however, was frightened, and she begged her nursemaid to stop. Tituba was very fond of Betty and did as she asked. But Mary was now intrigued. Like any girl her age, Mary wanted to know if there was a sweetheart in her future. Could Tituba tell fortunes?

*This print from the 1800s shows Tituba telling
a tale to the girls in the Parris kitchen.*

Of course, fortune-telling was a sin in the Puritan community
of Salem Village. Only recently, the Reverend Samuel Parris had
given a sermon about the evils of it. Still, it was a common enough
practice. For the young people, who were naturally curious about
the future, it offered a source of much-needed entertainment.

Tituba agreed to look into the future for Mary. Yes, there was
a young man ahead: "a fellow to the eastward." Mary was too ex-
cited to keep the news to herself. On her way home, she told her

friend Elizabeth Booth. Naturally, Elizabeth wanted to be included in the next fortune-telling session.

News of Tituba's talents continued to be whispered to other girls living farther away from the parsonage. Four maidservants joined the group in the parsonage kitchen: seventeen-year-old Elizabeth Hubbard, who served the home of her uncle, Dr. William Griggs; twenty-year-old Sarah Churchill, servant to George Jacobs; twenty-year-old Mary Warren, who had developed a crush on her master, John Proctor; and nineteen-year-old Mercy Lewis, servant to the Putnam family. They all became members of the secret circle. But none of them could keep a secret.

Ann Putnam, Mercy Lewis's mistress, was given to having nightmares. It was always the same dream. Her sister had died recently, as had her sister's babies. Her own baby had also died in its cradle. Night after night she dreamed of the babies and her sister, wrapped in their winding sheets, calling to her to justify their murders. But Goody Putnam did not know who could have murdered her baby, her sister, and her sister's children. Then one day her servant, Mercy Lewis, returned from the parsonage with a tale of Tituba's talents. Goody Putnam wanted to know if Tituba could see into the past as well as the future. She sent her eldest daughter and namesake to the parsonage to find out. Twelve-year-old Ann Putnam was to become the ringleader of the "circle girls."

THE SECRET SEANCES continued, and they began to put a strain on nine-year-old Betty Parris. Betty spent hours staring, transfixed, into the fire. She began to act strangely at evening prayers. Rather than recite her prayers along with the rest of the family, Betty spewed forth jibberish. Only Tituba could recognize the words as a chant from her native West Indian tongue.

Betty's cousin Abigail was behaving oddly as well. She ran about the house flapping her arms and trying to fly, shouting, "Whish! Whish!" She even attempted to fly up the chimney, scattering hot coals everywhere.

Reverend Parris prayed over the children, but they did not improve. After a month of this behavior he called in a doctor. The doctor examined both girls but could find nothing physically wrong with them. "The evil hand is upon them," he said.

Reverend Parris prepared a special Sunday service. He informed his congregation that he would read from Michael Wigglesworth's *Day of Doom*. This was a very popular work among the Puritans. They read it almost as often as the Bible itself. Still, it was unusual to read from anything other than Holy Scripture for Sunday service. What could be the minister's meaning? Could it have something to do with Betty and Abigail? The whole village knew of their strange illness. They were soon to have their answer.

As her father began his reading, Betty became restless. He thundered a passage:

Forthwith he cries, Ye Dead arise,
And unto Judgement come.
No sooner said, but 'tis obey'd
Sepulchers open'd are;
Dead Bodies all rise at his call . . .

Betty could bear her guilt no longer. She had heard her father practice his speech at home. She shrieked the next passage, drowning out her father's rumbling tones:

The pious father had now much rather
His graceless son should lie
In Hell with Devils, for all his sins
Burning eternally . . .

[33]

The Day of Doom was written by Michael Wigglesworth, an American minister, in 1662. It contained vivid images from the Bible and was very popular among the Puritans.

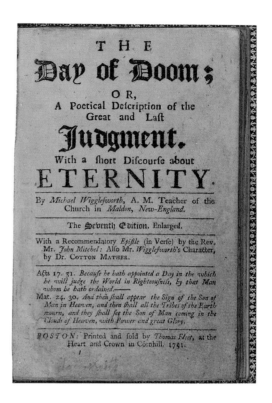

Then she collapsed in a fit.

Betty's fit spread like wildfire to the other girls from the parsonage kitchen séances. Young Ann Putnam began to choke. Mary Walcott and Elizabeth Booth started babbling. Abigail dropped to her hands and knees and followed her aunt and cousin out of the meetinghouse on all fours, barking like a dog.

This kind of behavior, where the many pick up the symptoms and mannerisms of one, is known as mass hysteria. It is brought on by intense anxiety and emotional instability. The imagined illness is real enough to those who experience it, although little harm is usually done. In Salem in 1692, the effects of the girls' hysterical fits were disastrous.

*T*HERE WAS NO HIDING the situation now. News of this mass fit spread almost as fast as the girls' convulsions. The Reverend Nicholas Noyes, minister of the First Church of Salem in Salem Town, came to examine the girls, as did all the ministers of the North Shore. These learned men were certain that the souls of these youngsters were in terrible danger. It was part of the Puritan belief that the Devil would try to take over the religious community of the faithful by corrupting its children. A day of fasting and prayer was declared, in hope of ridding the girls of their dreadful demons.

But the more these ministers prayed over the girls, the worse their seizures became. This did not surprise the ministers. The information they had in their European books on witchcraft, books like the *Malleus Maleficarum,* described exactly this behavior. There was only one thing to do: identify those who afflicted the girls, bring them to Puritan justice, and save not only the souls of these young people but the future of the Puritan community as well.

"Who afflicts thee, dear child?" they asked. The girls did not know how to answer. They were bewildered by so much attention. Again and again the question was put to them. "Dear child, who is it? Who are these wicked ones?" Still the girls remained silent. But the ministers persisted. They knew that God did not permit his followers to be afflicted by the Devil without opening the eyes of the victims to the ones who tormented them.

The people of Salem Village began looking among themselves for likely candidates. Well-meaning neighbors asked, "Does Goody Osburne afflict thee? Does Goody Good?" Finally, giving in to the constant pressure, the girls "cried out" these very names and a third: Tituba.

On February 29, 1692, warrants were issued for the arrest of these three women. The Salem witchcraft trials had begun.

5

THE
EXAMINATIONS

It surprised no one in Salem Village when Sarah Good was named as a witch. She was a troublesome character and not particularly liked. She had been married three times; her last husband, William Good, had deserted her. She now lived as a beggar with her children, combing the Salem Village streets for handouts. When she was denied charity, she was known to walk away muttering fiercely to herself and cursing those who refused her. Still worse, Sarah was never seen at Sunday meetings.

Sarah Osburne was of a completely different character than Goody Good. But she managed to get herself gossiped about. Sarah had been widowed and had continued to live on her small farm in the company of her late husband's overseer, Alexander Osburne. She had eventually married the man, but her earlier behavior had set tongues wagging. She also seemed to have frequent quarrels with her neighbors.

[36]

Goody Good, Goody Osburne, and Tituba were brought to the village meetinghouse to be questioned. Goody Osburne, who had long been bedridden, had to be helped into the meetinghouse to stand before Judges John Hathorne and Jonathan Corwin. These two men had ridden over from Salem Town to conduct the hearing. From this examination, they would determine whether Goody Good and Goody Osburne should be held over for trial.

The "circle girls" had been stationed in the meetinghouse before the three women were led in. Of the group, only Betty Parris was not there.

The villagers crammed into the meetinghouse to watch the proceedings. Judge Hathorne began by asking Sarah Good if she had made a contract with the Devil. She answered no.

HATHORNE: Why do you hurt these children?
GOOD: I do not hurt them. I scorn it.
HATHORNE: Whom do you employ, then, to do it?
GOOD: I employ nobody.
HATHORNE: What creature do you employ, then?
GOOD: No creature, but I am falsely accused.
HATHORNE: Why did you go away muttering from Mr. Parris his house?
GOOD: I did not mutter but I thanked him for what he gave my child. [Five-year-old Dorcas]

Judge Hathorne then asked the "circle girls" to look at Sarah Good and tell him if this was the person who had hurt them. The girls did as they were instructed and said that Sarah Good was, indeed, one of the persons that injured them. Then they fell on the floor screaming as if they were being tormented. Their arms and legs jerked in convulsions, and they foamed at the mouth.

[37]

HATHORNE:	Sarah Good, do you not see now what you have done? Why do you not tell us the truth? Why do you thus torment these poor children?
GOOD:	I do not torment them.
HATHORNE:	How came they thus tormented?
GOOD:	I do not know but it was some[one] you brought into the meetinghouse with you.
HATHORNE:	We brought you into the meetinghouse.
GOOD:	But you brought in two more.
HATHORNE:	Who was it then that tormented the children?

Sarah Good now weakened under the judge's attack.

GOOD:	It was Osburne.

Sarah Osburne was questioned next. She was quite weak, having been so long in her sickbed. The questions began again.

HATHORNE:	What evil spirit have you familiarity with?
OSBURNE:	None.
HATHORNE:	Have you made no contract with the Devil?
OSBURNE:	No. I never saw the Devil in my life.
HATHORNE:	Why do you hurt these children?
OSBURNE:	I do not hurt them.
HATHORNE:	What familiarity have you with Sarah Good?
OSBURNE:	None. I have not seen her these two years.

As with Sarah Good, Judge Hathorne asked the "circle girls" to stand and look at Sarah Osburne. They did and performed in exactly the same way they had before—rolling on the floor, their bodies twisted in some kind of strange fit.

[38]

The accusation of two "witches" at Salem.

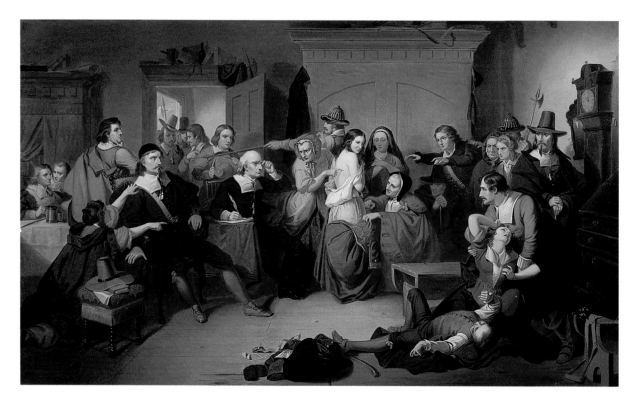

Officials examine a woman accused of witchcraft. A mole
or birthmark could be considered a "witch's mark"
—proof that the accused was in league with the Devil.

Finally Tituba was brought in. When the girls saw her, their "torment" became even more spectacular. Tituba was beyond being frightened. The Reverend Parris had questioned her at home. Not receiving the answer he wanted on the cause of his daughter Betty's affliction, he had beaten Tituba until she confessed to witchcraft. She was now prepared to do the same before the magistrates.

HATHORNE:	Did you never see the Devil?
TITUBA:	The Devil came to me and bid me serve him.
HATHORNE:	Who have you seen?
TITUBA:	Four women sometimes hurt the children.
HATHORNE:	Who were they?
TITUBA:	Goody Osburne and Sarah Good. I do not know who the others were. Sarah Good and Sarah Osburne would have me hurt the children.

As the questioning continued, Tituba described how she had been visited by a strange vision that sometimes took the form of a man and sometimes the form of a beast.

HATHORNE:	What is this appearance you see?
TITUBA:	Sometimes it is like a hog and sometimes like a great dog.
HATHORNE:	What did it say to you?
TITUBA:	The black dog said serve me, but I said I am afraid. He said if I did not [serve him] he would do worse to me.
HATHORNE:	What did you say to it?
TITUBA:	I will serve you no longer. This man had a yellow bird . . . and he told me he had more pretty things that he would give me if I would serve him.
HATHORNE:	What were these pretty things?
TITUBA:	He did not show me them.
HATHORNE:	Why did you go to Thomas Putnam's last night and hurt his child?
TITUBA:	They pull and haul me and make go.

HATHORNE:	And what would [they] have you do?
TITUBA:	Kill her with a knife.
HATHORNE:	How did you go?
TITUBA:	We ride upon sticks.
HATHORNE:	What attendants [familiars] hath Sarah Good?
TITUBA:	A yellow bird.
HATHORNE:	What meat did she give it?
TITUBA:	It did suck her between her fingers.
HATHORNE:	What hath Sarah Osburne?
TITUBA:	Yesterday, she had a thing with a head like a woman with two legs and wings. Abigail Williams that lives with her uncle, Mr. Parris, said that she did see this same creature and it turned into the shape of Goody Osburne.

With this much "evidence" against Goody Good and Goody Os-burne, the judges thought they should hold both of them over for trial. They were carted off to jail. Tituba, because she had con-fessed, would not be tried but was taken to jail until the magis-trates could decide what was to be done with her.

THE EXAMINATIONS of Sarah Good, Sarah Osburne, and Tituba took place at the beginning of March 1692. However, there were no actual trials until June of that year. This was because Sal-em's original charter, granted by the British Crown, had been re-voked. In the spring of 1692, Salem was actually operating without a government, and no court could hold session until a new charter was established.

This situation contributed to a general feeling of uncertainty among the citizens of both town and village. Without laws, title to the very farms they worked was in question. In times of uncertainty, it is not uncommon for people to look for a "scapegoat," someone or some group to blame for their problems. It is likely that the unstable atmosphere in Salem helped ignite the witch-hunt. The girls' accusations were like a match tossed on kindling.

A new governor, William Phips, disembarked from the ship *Nonesuch* in May 1692 and walked straight into the chaos of the Salem witch-hunt. Already, the jails of Salem Town, Ipswich, and Boston were overflowing with accused witches. Phips reported to their majesties William and Mary in England, "I found this Province miserably harassed with a most Horrible witchcraft or Possession of Devills."

The new governor wasted no time. On May 27, he established the Court of "Oyer and Terminer," a Latin term meaning "to hear and determine." This court was to try the cases of those who had been accused of witchcraft.

Governor Phips handpicked the judges. The chief justice was Lieutenant Governor William Stoughton. He was a firm believer in the existence of witches and was determined to rid the land of them. Samuel Sewall was known to be an honest man but weak. He was horrified at the turn of events the trials took but did not have the courage to object. Major Bartholomew Gedney was a brave man who had fought in the Indian wars and was a doctor by profession. Other judges were John Richards, Wait Winthrop, and Peter Sergeant. None of these three had qualifications to become judges, other than coming from respected families. They certainly had no knowledge of legal procedure.

Left: William Stoughton, chief justice for the trials. Right: Samuel Sewall, a judge.

The home of Jonathan Corwin, a Salem Town magistrate, was the scene of some of the hearings.

The local judge from Salem Town, John Hathorne, was kept on and conducted most of the questioning. Like Chief Justice Stoughton, Hathorne staunchly believed in witchcraft. He presumed all of the accused were guilty even before they were tried. He also refused to allow anyone to speak on behalf of the prisoners. So central was Hathorne's role in the prosecution and persecution of the Salem witches that, three generations later, Hathorne's great-grandson, novelist Nathaniel Hawthorne, changed the spelling of his last name so as not to be associated with his notorious great-grandfather.

Also appointed was Major General Nathaniel Saltonstall. He was an odd choice because he did not share Puritan beliefs. He also did not last long on the bench: He resigned after the first hanging. He was replaced by Jonathan Corwin. Corwin was a rum dealer by trade and a weak man. He became little more than a mouthpiece for Hathorne.

With the Court of Oyer and Terminer appointed, the actual trials were ready to begin. On April 18, a warrant for the arrest of Bridget Bishop had been sworn out by Abigail Williams, Mercy Lewis, Ann Putnam, Reverend Samuel Parris, Nathaniel Ingersoll, Thomas Putnam, Mary Walcott, and Elizabeth Hubbard. Goody Bishop's trial, which began on June 2, became the first of the Salem witchcraft trials. Twelve years earlier, she had been accused of witchcraft, tried, and released. She would not fare so well this time.

6

THE TRIALS
BEGIN

The earlier charge of witchcraft aside, Goody Bishop's reputation was generally bad. She ran a drinking house on the road between Salem and the neighboring community of Beverly. Bridget Bishop dressed loudly. She wore a red bodice laced with many-colored ribbons as she served her customers their rum and beer. The godly people of Salem took offense at her dress and her business, which was little more than a bawdy, drunken bar. Many times the church had taken her to task for keeping the tavern open so late at night. She was in her sixties and had been widowed twice. She was now married to Edward Bishop, who, during the course of her trial, was only too glad to testify against her.

As in the earlier examinations, the "circle girls" were present at the trial. Rumors and gossip figured heavily in the questioning:

HATHORNE: They say you bewitched your first husband to death.
BISHOP: If it please your worship, I know nothing of it.

When Bridget Bishop shook her head or moved in any way, the girls imitated her movement and screamed with "affliction."

HATHORNE: Why [do] you seem to act witchcraft before us by the motion of your body, which seems to have influence upon the afflicted?
BISHOP: I know nothing of it. I am innocent . . . I know not what a witch is.
HATHORNE: How can you know you are no witch and yet not know what a witch is?
BISHOP: I am clear. If I were any such person you should know it.

Judge Hathorne then spoke to the girls.

HATHORNE: Look upon this woman and see if this be the woman that you have seen hurting you.

The "afflicted" again began having their fits, writhing on the floor.

HATHORNE: What do you say now you see they charge you to your face?
BISHOP: I never did hurt them in my life. I did never see these persons before. I am as innocent as the child unborn.
LEWIS: Oh Goody Bishop, did you not come to our house the last night and did you not tell me that your master made you tell more than you were willing to tell?

[47]

HATHORNE: Tell us the truth in this matter. How come these persons to be thus tormented and to charge you with doing?

BISHOP: I am not come here to say I am a witch to take away my life.

The most important issue in the Salem witchcraft trials was the admission of "spectral evidence," the supposed visions of the "afflicted." By admitting spectral evidence, the court allowed the accused to be convicted on nothing more than dreams, fantasies, and hallucinations. Spectral evidence was "proved" by the fact that it could not be disproved. Soon older members of the community picked up on the girls' "visions" and invented some of their own. Thirty-six-year-old William Stacy, for example, offered testimony against Bridget Bishop.

> *In the winter, about midnight, [Stacy] felt something between his lips, pressing hard against his teeth. And withall, [he] was very cold in so much that it did awake[n] him so that he got up and sat upon his bed, he, at the same time seeing the said Bridget Bishop sitting at the foot of his bed. . . . It was then as light as if it had been day. . . . Then she, the said Bishop or her shape, clapped her coat close to her legs and hopped upon the bed and about the room and then went out.*

Bridget Bishop was convicted on this evidence on June 8. On June 10, she was hanged.

The next trials scheduled were those of Sarah Good and Sarah Osburne. Sarah Osburne never came to trial, however. She was already frail from her long illness, and being chained in jail had not improved her health. She had died in prison on May 10.

Ann Putnam's sworn state-ment against Sarah Good.

A bottle containing "witch pins" that witches were said to use to torture victims.

The trial of Sarah Good did go forward. Ann Putnam, leader of the "circle girls," offered evidence against her:

On the 25th of February . . . I saw the apparition of Sarah Good which did torture me most grievous[ly]. But I did not know her name until the 27th of February. And then she told me her name was Sarah Good. And then she did prick me and pinch me most grievous[ly] and also since several times.

[49]

Elizabeth Hubbard also testified against Sarah Good. Her statement directly mirrored that of Ann Putnam. Then Sarah Good's five-year-old daughter, Dorcas, was brought in to testify against her mother. Ann Putnam, Mercy Lewis, and Mary Walcott all stated that the "shape" of little Dorcas had "afflicted" them by pinching and biting. During her questioning, Dorcas said that her mother had made her a witch and that her mother "had three birds, one black and one yellow, and that these birds hurt the children and afflicted persons.

Little Dorcas was taken to jail and put in chains. There she stayed until the trials were over and all remaining prisoners were released, in the spring of 1693. She was never the same after her imprisonment. For the rest of her life, she behaved like a hunted animal.

Sarah Good was hanged on July 19. Her husband, Edward, all too gladly followed her cart to the gallows. He remarried shortly after Sarah's execution.

No one in Salem Village was surprised by the convictions of these people. Nor were they particularly sorry to see them hang. But suddenly the nature of the trials changed. The girls now "cried out against" one of the most pious and godly of the entire Salem community: Ann Putnam named Martha Corey as a witch.

7

THE DEVIL'S INSTRUMENTS

Martha Corey was a stout countrywoman and a devout believer in the Puritan faith. She was also outspoken, and her directness frequently irritated her fellow church members. Martha had become a member of the Salem Village church only in the last year. Before that, she had been a member of the church in Salem Town.

Martha differed from her Puritan fellows in that she did not believe in witches. When her eighty-one-year-old husband, Giles, planned to attend the trials, she asked him not to go and, by his presence, support such foolishness. He was quite determined to go, however, so Martha hid his saddle. This was viewed with suspicion by her neighbors.

After Ann Putnam identified her as a witch, two court officials, Ezekiel Cheever and Edward Putnam, went to interview Martha Corey privately. Before they left, they asked Ann to look closely at Martha's spectral shape and describe what clothes she was wear-ing. Ann was not able to do this, claiming that the witch had cast a spell on her.

When the two men arrived at Martha Corey's house, she looked at them and smiled. "I know what you have come for," she said. "You are come to talk to me about being a witch." If they had any doubt that Martha was indeed a witch, she destroyed it by her next statement: "Did she tell you what clothes I have on? Well, did she tell you?"

Actually, there was nothing mysterious in Martha's state-ments. It was only too easy to guess what the errand was when two officials from the Court of Oyer and Terminer stood on her door-step. It was also widely known that the girls were asked to describe the clothes worn by the accused's spectral shape. But Martha Corey was brought before the magistrates and questioned closely.

HATHORNE: Who told you about the clothes? Why did you ask that question?

COREY: Because I heard the children told what clothes the other[s] wore.

HATHORNE: You dare thus to lie in all this assembly. You are now before Authority. I expect the truth. You promised it. Speak now and tell. . . . Who told you what clothes?

COREY: Nobody.

HATHORNE: How do you know what they came for? Answer me this truly.

COREY: I had heard speech that the children said I . . . troubled them and I thought that they might come to examine [me].

CHILD:	There is a man whispering in her ear!
HATHORNE:	What did he say to you?
COREY:	We must not believe all that these distracted children say.

At this point, the children screamed and howled.

HATHORNE:	Here dare more than two that accuse you . . . What do you say?
COREY:	What can I do? Many rise up against me.
HATHORNE:	Why, confess.
COREY:	So I would if I were guilty.

For all her good intention of bringing people to their senses by her testimony, Martha Corey only got herself in deeper trouble. The "circle girls," by their convulsions, convinced the judges. An accused person had no chance against them. Martha Corey was found guilty and was executed on September 22.

*D*URING Martha Corey's examination, the name of Rebecca Nurse was brought up several times. The day after Martha's questioning, a warrant was issued for Rebecca's arrest. Rebecca was known throughout Salem as a pious person. Hearing her "cried out" as a witch shocked the people of both Salem Town and Salem Village. However, there was a strong undercurrent running against not just Rebecca, but the entire Nurse family.

Years earlier, Rebecca and her husband, Francis, had agreed to purchase three hundred acres from the Endicott family. Rebecca's four sons, and her sons-in-law from the marriages of her four

Torture at Salem

COMPARED WITH European practices, the methods used to obtain confessions from accused witches during the Salem trials would be considered mild. "Pricking" a "witch's mark" was common, as was torturing the prisoner's family. Several children of the accused witches were tortured to obtain evidence against their parents.

The cruelest method of torture used in the Salem trials was inflicted on Giles Corey. Corey had been tricked into testifying against his wife, Martha. When he protested her treatment, he was promptly accused of witchcraft himself. Under English law at this time, a person could not be tried without entering a plea of "guilty" or "innocent." But Corey refused to enter a plea.

In their frustration, the judges ordered him pressed until he agreed to confess. When an individual was pressed, he or she was tied to stakes in the ground. A board was placed lengthwise on the victim, and heavy rocks were then loaded on the board. More weight was added, crushing the unfortunate person beneath until he or she confessed. Giles Corey uttered only two words during his ordeal: "More weight." Then he died.

Giles Corey refused to enter a plea in court.

daughters, all worked the farm to pay off the purchase in twenty annual installments. There were people in Salem Village who frowned on this kind of behavior. Old Francis was a tray maker by trade and, they felt, should have remained as such. Instead, the Nurses had become prosperous farmers.

Then there was the time one of the neighbor's hogs got into Rebecca's flax garden. It was one of those rare occasions when Rebecca lost her temper. She drove the hogs out of her garden, all the while cursing her neighbor. Shortly after this incident, the neighbor died. Now, in the light of the witch-hunt, this looked like more than coincidence.

There had also been a disagreement with Thomas Putnam over a property line. No doubt young Ann had heard her parents discuss the matter around the house. It was Ann who led the accusations against Rebecca Nurse, crying out at Rebecca's trial that she was hurting her.

JUDGE: Goody Nurse, here are two, Ann Putnam, the child, and Abigail Williams [who] complain of your hurting them. What do you say to it?

NURSE: I can say before my Eternal Father I am innocent.

Judge Hathorne had been moved to pity when Rebecca Nurse was brought to the bar for examination. She was seventy-one years old, and the years had made her hard of hearing. She was also weak from a recent illness and could barely stand. Hathorne was aware of Rebecca's good reputation and wanted to find her innocent.

HATHORNE: Here is never a one in the assembly but desires it. But if you be guilty, pray God discover you.

NURSE:	I am innocent and clear and have not been able to get out of doors these eight or nine days. I never afflicted no child, never in my life.

At this point, Goody Putnam called out against Rebecca Nurse. She still believed that witchcraft was behind the deaths of her baby, her sister, and her sister's children, and she was determined that someone be punished.

"Oh, Lord, help me," responded Rebecca—and, as she spread out her hands in prayer, the "afflicted" again enacted their "torment," claiming that they saw a yellow bird flying above her.

HATHORNE:	Do you not see what a solemn condition these [people] are in? When your hands are loose the persons are afflicted.
NURSE:	The Lord knows I have not hurt them. I am an innocent person.

At this point, Judge Hathorne began to doubt Rebecca's innocence. She did not cry during her examination. The common belief of the day was that a witch was not capable of shedding tears.

HATHORNE:	It is very awful to all to see these agonies and you . . . stand with dry eyes when there are so many wet.
NURSE:	You do not know my heart.

At first, the jury returned a verdict of not guilty. The girls went into screaming fits at the news. Chief Justice Stoughton sent the jury back to reconsider. This time they found Rebecca Nurse guilty.

The Nurse family petitioned Governor Phips to have her sentence overturned, and he granted the reprieve. But, hearing that Rebecca had been released, Ann Putnam "lay like death" in a coma. The governor canceled his reprieve, and Rebecca was hanged on July 19. Ann recovered with the news of the hanging.

THE AFTERNOON OF Rebecca's examination, the Reverend Deodat Lawson of Boston had given a sermon to the faithful of troubled Salem. The good people of Salem Village had been wondering how the most godly of them could have become instruments of the Devil. Lawson assured them that if the Devil's purpose was to overtake the community of the faithful, he would certainly choose those who were outwardly holy and devout, "for it is certain that [Satan] never works more like the Prince of Darkness than when he looks most like an angel of light."

Still, there were those who thought the whole procedure a sham. John Proctor was one. His serving girl, Mary Warren, was one of the "circle girls." Proctor, however, thought very little of her "afflictions." "If they are let alone," he said, "we should all be devils and witches." He had a better solution to Mary's convulsions: He plunked her down in front of her spinning wheel and forbade her to move from it. Away from the other girls in the group, Mary's fits stopped. But Proctor had been very vocal in his objections to the proceedings, and the damage had already been done. And, like the Nurse family, John Proctor had had arguments with some of his neighbors.

On April 11, Proctor's wife, Elizabeth, was arrested. When he protested her treatment in court, he was led away in chains. As Proctor was the wealthiest of those accused, the sheriff wasted no time in seizing his property. Usually, this would not happen until the accused witch had been tried and found guilty.

The "evidence" against Proctor was the same "evidence" used against the other "witches." Abigail Williams, Ann Putnam, Mercy Lewis, and Proctor's servant, Mary Warren, all testified that the spectral shape of John Proctor had tormented them "by pinching, twisting, and almost choking them." The fact that Proctor had kept Mary Warren away from some of the earlier trials no doubt weighed against him. He was found guilty and was hanged on August 19.

Elizabeth Proctor was condemned, but because she was pregnant her hanging was postponed until after she had the baby. By that time, the witch-hunt was over, and her life was spared.

Also executed on August 19 was the Reverend George Burroughs. He had once been a minister in Salem Village but had left under bad circumstances. For one thing, he had had a disagreement with Thomas Putnam over a debt. Burroughs was practicing his ministry in Boston when Ann Putnam "cried against" him as a witch. He was brought back to Salem in chains to stand trial.

He was quickly convicted. At his execution, he was allowed to speak, and he spoke so well that many in the crowd were moved to tears. He concluded by reciting the Lord's Prayer perfectly. The crowd began to stir. Was this not the true test? Then Cotton Mather, a young author and "scientist" of witchcraft, swung into his saddle and rode through the crowd, reminding them of Reverend Lawson's sermon. The Devil was most himself when he appeared otherwise, Mather said. Burroughs was not what he appeared. Neither was he a properly ordained minister. This quieted the crowd long enough for the executioner to do his job.

But this incident did cause some of the people of Salem to question the methods used in the trials.

The execution of George Burroughs, a respected minister,
caused many people to question the Salem trials.

8

THE TRIALS END

By October, the witchcraft "disease" had spread to the neighboring communities of Beverly, Andover, and Gloucester. Some people in Gloucester, in fact, considered their town so infested with witches that they invited the "circle girls" to come and identify the witches that were plaguing them.

The girls were escorted by a Salem constable. As they crossed the bridge into Ipswich, they came upon an old woman. Immediately, the girls fell into fits, howling that this woman was a witch. However, a strange thing happened: nothing. Those standing nearby made no move either to help the girls or to arrest the woman. Instead, they directed the constable to take the "wenches" elsewhere. Ipswich was the birthplace of Goodman John Proctor, and the citizens of that town had signed a petition to have his sentence overturned. Of course, that had been denied, and Proctor had been hanged. But the people of Ipswich wanted no part of these "visionary maids," as the girls were sometimes called.

Things went little better for the girls in Gloucester. Only a handful of people had invited them. The majority of Gloucester's citizens doubted the girls' abilities to identify witches and gave them a cold reception. Having grown used to the awe and reverence given them by the people of Salem, the girls were distracted by the rudeness they found waiting for them in Gloucester. They were unable to name any witches. Mercy Lewis, however, persisted and "cried out" the wife of a local magistrate. The woman was much respected within the community. Mercy Lewis was told she was mistaken. The girls were sent back to Salem.

By now, several petitions had reached Governor Phips concerning the use of spectral evidence. Increase Mather, president of Harvard College, had escorted the new governor when he had journeyed to America in May. He now called the governor's attention to the fact that court officials had obtained confessions by torture and threat of death. There was also concern that confessing witches seemed to accuse others as the court needed. And there was the increasing number of the "afflicted." If real witches were being jailed and executed, the number of people being harmed by witchcraft should be going down, not up.

But the girls continued to name witches. They "cried out" against the minister John Hale's wife. They named former Judge Saltonstall a witch. Then they "cried out" against Lady Phips, Governor Phips's wife. Now they had gone too far. The Court of Oyer and Terminer adjourned on September 24, 1692. It would never meet again.

*B*Y THE SPRING OF 1693, the governor had released all prisoners still being held in the crowded prisons of Salem and surrounding towns. The Salem witchcraft trials were over, but the stain on the reputations of the accused, both dead and surviving, remained.

In 1702 the General Court of Massachusetts declared the witchcraft proceedings of 1692 and the use of spectral evidence illegal. They did nothing to clear the names of the accused, condemned, and executed, however. Elizabeth Proctor, for example, was freed in the "general delivery" of 1693 but was technically still a condemned woman awaiting an execution date. In 1709, a group of surviving "witches" and family members of victims petitioned the General Court to not only clear the names of those accused but to grant financial compensation to them as well. By and large, these requests were granted within a few years. However, those like Bridget Bishop who had been executed and had no family left to plead for them remained on the books as condemned witches. The names of these unfortunate people would not be cleared until 1957.

And what happened to those who had placed the noose around the necks of the innocent? On January 15, 1697, former judge Samuel Sewall and those who had participated as jurors begged forgiveness of the families of the hanged "witches." In 1706, Ann Putnam stood before the Puritan congregation and begged to "lie in the dust and be humbled" for her role in the Salem witchcraft trials. As for the other "circle girls," two fell into ill repute, and several moved away. The others married and, by taking their husbands' last names, all too gladly distanced themselves from the upheaval of their adolescence.

Regni *ANNÆ* Reginæ Decimo.

Province of the Massachusetts-Bay.

AN ACT,

Made and Passed by the Great and General Court or Assembly of Her Majesty's Province of the Massachusetts-Bay in New-England, Held at Boston the 17th Day of October, 1711.

An Act to Reverse the Attainders of *George Burroughs* and others for Witchcraft.

FORASMUCH as in the Year of our Lord One Thousand Six Hundred Ninety Two, Several Towns within this Province were Infested with a horrible Witchcraft or Possession of Devils ; And at a Special Court of Oyer and Terminer holden at Salem, in the County of Essex in the same Year One Thousand Six Hundred Ninety Two, George Burroughs *of Wells,* John Procter, George Jacob, John Willard, Giles Core, *and his Wife,* Rebecca Nurse, *and* Sarah Good, *all of Salem aforesaid* : Elizabeth How, *of Ipswich,* Mary Eastey, Sarah Wild *and* Abigail Hobbs *all of Topsfield* : Samuel Wardell, Mary Parker, Martha Carrier, Abigail Falkner, Anne Foster, Rebecca Eames, Mary Post, *and* Mary Lacey, *all of Andover* : Mary Bradbury *of Salisbury :* and Dorcas Hoar *of Beverly ; Were severally Indicted, Convicted and Attained of Witchcraft, and some of them put to Death, Others lying still under the like Sentence of the said Court, and liable to have the same Executed upon them.*

A   The

The Salem witchcraft trials were the last true, large-scale witch-hunt, in which victims were accused of flying on broomsticks and sending their "shapes" to hurt others. But there have been other "witch-hunts" since 1692. We see the same thought patterns (or lack of thought) any time one group of people blames another for its problems and persecutes that group. Rather than carefully thinking things through, it would seem that human nature prefers to point the finger at someone else. This can happen on a small scale as well as a large one. As can be seen by the example of Salem, it happens among children as well as adults.

In every classroom, there is always one child who is shut out by the rest of his or her classmates. No one looks closely as to why this child is set apart from the rest. He or she is different, and that is all it takes to "condemn" him or her. If another member of the class tries to befriend the outcast, that child then finds him- or herself cast out as well. Children who are different today may not be "cried out" as witches like five-year-old Dorcas Good in Salem, but the effect upon the excluded classmate can be damaging.

Like the emperor who wasn't wearing any clothes, in the fable by Hans Christian Andersen, people often do not like to hear the truth about themselves. It is much simpler to place the blame elsewhere. This situation can easily get out of control. It did in Salem Village in 1692.

Chronology

1626	Founding of Salem Town.
1630s	Puritans arrive from England.
	Salem Village begins as a settlement.
1672	Salem Village becomes a separate parish of Salem Town.
1674	Salem Village builds its own meetinghouse.
1691	November: The séances begin in the Parris kitchen.
1692	February: Witchcraft accusations and arrests begin.
	June to September: Witchcraft trials and executions.
	September 24: Court of Oyer and Terminer meets for the last time.
1693	May: General "jail delivery"; those remaining in prison are granted pardons and released.
1711	The General Court of Massachusetts clears the names of those "witches" who survived or those deceased who had families to plead for them.
1957	The names of the last of the executed are cleared.

Further Reading

Fradin, Dennis B. *The Massachusetts Colony*. Chicago: Childrens Press, 1986.

Garden, Nancy. *Witches*. Philadelphia: J. B. Lippincott Company, 1975.

Jackson, Shirley. *Witchcraft of Salem Village*. New York: Random House, 1956.

Petry, Ann. *Tituba of Salem Village*. New York: Harper & Row Junior Books, 1988.

Revesz, Therese R. *Witches*. Milwaukee, Wis.: Raintree, 1977.

Stallman, Birdie. *Learning About Witches*. Chicago: Childrens Press, 1981.

Zeinert, Karen. *The Salem Witchcraft Trials*. New York: Franklin Watts, 1989.

Bibliography

The quotations that appear in the accounts of the Salem witchcraft trials in this book are drawn from the trial transcripts, which are on file at the Essex Institute in Salem, Massachusetts, and have been collected and published in several works.

Spellings and some punctuation have been updated to make these passages more understandable to modern readers. Other sources consulted include the following:

Beard, George Miller. *The Psychology of the Salem Witch Trials*. New York: G.P. Putnam's Sons, 1882.

Boyer, Paul, and Nissenbaum, Stephen. *Salem Possessed*. Cambridge: Harvard University Press, 1974.

Boyer, Paul, and Nissenbaum, Stephen. *The Salem Witchcraft Papers*, Volumes I, II, III. New York: Da Capo Press, 1977.

Bradley, Marion Zimmer. *The Mists of Avalon*. New York: Alfred A. Knopf, 1983.

Briggs, Katherine M. *Nine Lives: The Folklore of Cats*. New York: Pantheon Books, 1980.

Garden, Nancy. *Witches*. Philadelphia: J.B. Lippincott Company, 1975.

Gemmill, William Nelson. *The Salem Witch Trials*. Chicago: A.C. McClure and Co., 1924.

Grun, Bernard. *The Timetables of History*. New York: Simon and Schuster, 1975.

Guiley, Rosemary Ellen. *The Encyclopedia of Witches and Witchcraft*. New York: Facts on File, 1989.

Karlsen, Carol F. *The Devil in the Shape of a Woman*. New York: Vintage Books, 1989.

Lethbridge, T.C. *Witches*. New York: The Citadel Press, 1982.

Miller, Arthur. *The Crucible*. New York: The Viking Press, 1971.

Rolleston, T.W. *Myths and Legends of the Celtic Race*. New York: Schocken Books, 1986.

Seth, Ronald. *Witches and Their Craft*. London: Odham Books, 1967.

Starky, Marion L. *The Devil in Massachusetts*. New York: Alfred A. Knopf, 1949.

Starky, Marion L. *The Visionary Girls*. Boston: Little, Brown and Company, 1973.

Upham, Charles W. *Salem Witchcraft*, Volumes I and II. New York: Frederick Unger Publishing Co., 1976.

Weisman, Richard. *Witchcraft Magic and Religion in the Seventeenth Century*. Amherst: The University of Andover Press, 1984.

Williams, Charles. *Witchcraft*. London: Faber and Faber Limited.

Index

Page numbers in *italics*
refer to illustrations.